The Key Facts™ on Afghanistan

Essential Information on Afghanistan

By Patrick W. Nee

The Internationalist®
www.internationalist.com

The Internationalist®

International Business, Investment, and Travel

Published by:

The Internationalist Publishing Company

96 Walter Street/ Suite 200

Boston, MA 02131, USA

Tel: 617-354-7722

www.internationalist.com

PN@internationalist.com

Copyright © 2013 by PWN

The Internationalist is a Registered Trademark. "Key Facts" and "The Internationalist Business Guides" are Trademarks of The Internationalist Publishing Company.

All Rights are reserved under International, Pan-American, and Pan-Asian Conventions. No part of this book may be reproduced in any form without the written permission of the publisher. All rights vigorously enforced

Table Of Contents

Chapter 1: Background

Chapter 2: Geography

Chapter 3: People and Society

Chapter 4: Government and Key Leaders

Chapter 5: Economy

Chapter 6: Energy

Chapter 7: Communications

Chapter 8: Transportation

Chapter 9: Military

Chapter 10: Transnational Issues

Map of Afghanistan

Chapter 1: Background

Ahmad Shah DURRANI unified the Pashtun tribes and founded Afghanistan in 1747. The country served as a buffer between the British and Russian Empires until it won independence from notional British control in 1919. A brief experiment in democracy ended in a 1973 coup and a 1978 Communist counter-coup. The Soviet Union invaded in 1979 to support the tottering Afghan Communist regime, touching off a long and destructive war. The USSR withdrew in 1989 under relentless pressure by internationally supported anti-Communist mujahedin rebels. A series of subsequent civil wars saw Kabul finally fall in 1996 to the Taliban, a hardline Pakistani-sponsored movement that emerged in 1994 to end the country's civil war and anarchy. Following the 11 September 2001 terrorist attacks, a US, Allied, and anti-Taliban Northern Alliance military action toppled the Taliban for sheltering Osama BIN LADIN. The UN-sponsored Bonn Conference in 2001 established a process for political reconstruction that included the adoption of a new constitution, a presidential election in 2004, and National Assembly elections in 2005. In December 2004, Hamid KARZAI became the first democratically elected president of Afghanistan and the National Assembly was inaugurated the following December. KARZAI was re-elected in August 2009 for a second term. Despite gains toward building a stable central government, a resurgent Taliban and continuing provincial instability - particularly in the south and the east - remain serious challenges for the Afghan Government.

Chapter 2: Geography

Location:
> Southern Asia, north and west of Pakistan, east of Iran

Geographic coordinates:
> 33 00 N, 65 00 E

Map references:
> Asia

Area:
> total: 652,230 sq km
> country comparison to the world: 41
> land: 652,230 sq km
> water: 0 sq km

Area - comparative:
> slightly smaller than Texas

Land boundaries:
> total: 5,529 km
> border countries: China 76 km, Iran 936 km, Pakistan 2,430 km, Tajikistan 1,206 km, Turkmenistan 744 km, Uzbekistan 137 km

Coastline:
> 0 km (landlocked)

Maritime claims:
> none (landlocked)

Climate:
> arid to semiarid; cold winters and hot summers

Terrain:

mostly rugged mountains; plains in north and southwest

Elevation extremes:
lowest point: Amu Darya 258 m
highest point: Noshak 7,485 m

Natural resources:
natural gas, petroleum, coal, copper, chromite, talc, barites, sulfur, lead, zinc, iron ore, salt, precious and semiprecious stones

Land use:
arable land: 12.13%
permanent crops: 0.21%
other: 87.66% (2005)

Irrigated land:
31,990 sq km (2003)

Total renewable water resources:
65 cu km (1997)

Freshwater withdrawal (domestic/industrial/agricultural):
total: 23.26 cu km/yr (2%/0%/98%)
per capita: 779 cu m/yr (2000)

Natural hazards:
damaging earthquakes occur in Hindu Kush mountains; flooding; droughts

Environment - current issues:
limited natural freshwater resources; inadequate supplies of potable water; soil degradation; overgrazing; deforestation (much of the remaining forests are being cut down for fuel and building materials); desertification; air and water pollution

Environment - international agreements:
>party to: Biodiversity, Climate Change, Desertification, Endangered Species, Environmental Modification, Marine Dumping, Ozone Layer Protection
>signed, but not ratified: Hazardous Wastes, Law of the Sea, Marine Life Conservation

Geography - note:
>landlocked; the Hindu Kush mountains that run northeast to southwest divide the northern provinces from the rest of the country; the highest peaks are in the northern Vakhan (Wakhan Corridor)

Chapter 3: People and Society

Nationality:
>noun: Afghan(s)
>adjective: Afghan

Ethnic groups:
>Pashtun 42%, Tajik 27%, Hazara 9%, Uzbek 9%, Aimak 4%, Turkmen 3%, Baloch 2%, other 4%

Languages:
>Afghan Persian or Dari (official) 50%, Pashto (official) 35%, Turkic languages (primarily Uzbek and Turkmen) 11%, 30 minor languages (primarily Balochi and Pashai) 4%, much bilingualism, but Dari functions as the lingua franca
>
>note: the Turkic languages Uzbek and Turkmen, as well as Balochi, Pashai, Nuristani, and Pamiri are the third official languages in areas where the majority speaks them

Religions:
>Sunni Muslim 80%, Shia Muslim 19%, other 1%

Population:
>31,108,077 (July 2013 est.)
>country comparison to the world: 40

Age structure:
>0-14 years: 43.2% (male 6,671,683/female 6,460,034)
>15-24 years: 21.6% (male 3,357,679/female 3,226,394)
>25-54 years: 28.9% (male 4,487,547/female 4,306,297)
>55-64 years: 3.8% (male 569,490/female 588,925)

65 years and over: 2.5% (male 350,692/female 401,187) (2012 est.)

Median age:
total: 17.9 years
male: 17.8 years
female: 17.9 years (2012 est.)

Population growth rate:
2.22% (2012 est.)
country comparison to the world: 41

Birth rate:
39.3 births/1,000 population (2012 est.)
country comparison to the world: 12

Death rate:
14.59 deaths/1,000 population (July 2012 est.)
country comparison to the world: 7

Net migration rate:
-2.51 migrant(s)/1,000 population (2012 est.)
country comparison to the world: 171

Urbanization:
urban population: 23% of total population (2010)
rate of urbanization: 4.7% annual rate of change (2010-15 est.)

Major cities - population:
KABUL (capital) 3.573 million (2009)

Sex ratio:
at birth: 1.05 male(s)/female
under 15 years: 1.03 male(s)/female

15-64 years: 1.04 male(s)/female

65 years and over: 0.87 male(s)/female

total population: 1.03 male(s)/female (2011 est.)

Maternal mortality rate:

460 deaths/100,000 live births (2010)

country comparison to the world: 21

Infant mortality rate:

total: 121.63 deaths/1,000 live births

country comparison to the world: 1

male: 129.51 deaths/1,000 live births

female: 113.36 deaths/1,000 live births (2012 est.)

Life expectancy at birth:

total population: 49.72 years

country comparison to the world: 218

male: 48.45 years

female: 51.05 years (2012 est.)

Total fertility rate:

5.54 children born/woman (2013 est.)

country comparison to the world: 8

Health expenditures:

7.6% of GDP (2010)

country comparison to the world: 70

Physicians density:

0.21 physicians/1,000 population (2009)

Hospital bed density:

0.4 beds/1,000 population (2010)

Drinking water source:
> Improved:
>> *urban*: 78% of population
>> *rural*: 42% of population
>> *total*: 50% of population
>
> Unimproved:
>> *urban*: 28% of population
>> *rural*: 58% of population
>> *total*: 50% of population (2010)

Sanitation facility access:
> Improved:
>> *urban*: 60% of population
>> *rural*: 30% of population
>> *total*: 37% of population
>
> Unimproved:
>> *urban*: 40% of population
>> *rural*: 70% of population
>> *total*: 63% of population (2010 est.)

HIV/AIDS - adult prevalence rate:
> 0.01% (2001 est.)
>
> country comparison to the world: 165

HIV/AIDS - people living with HIV/AIDS:
> NA

HIV/AIDS - deaths:
> NA

Major infectious diseases:

degree of risk: high
food or waterborne diseases: bacterial and protozoal diarrhea, hepatitis A, and typhoid fever
vectorborne disease: malaria
animal contact disease: rabies
note: highly pathogenic H5N1 avian influenza has been identified in this country; it poses a negligible risk with extremely rare cases possible among US citizens who have close contact with birds (2009)

Children under the age of 5 years underweight:
32.9% (2004)
country comparison to the world: 10

Education expenditures:
NA

Literacy:
definition: age 15 and over can read and write
total population: 28.1%
male: 43.1%
female: 12.6% (2000 est.)

School life expectancy (primary to tertiary education):
total: 9 years
male: 11 years
female: 7 years (2009)

Chapter 4: Government and Key Leaders

Country name:
> conventional long form: Islamic Republic of Afghanistan
> conventional short form: Afghanistan
> local long form: Jamhuri-ye Islami-ye Afghanistan
> local short form: Afghanistan
> former: Republic of Afghanistan

Government type:
> Islamic republic

Capital:
> name: Kabul
> geographic coordinates: 34 31 N, 69 11 E
> time difference: UTC+4.5 (9.5 hours ahead of Washington, DC during Standard Time)

Administrative divisions:
> 34 provinces (welayat, singular - welayat); Badakhshan, Badghis, Baghlan, Balkh, Bamyan, Daykundi, Farah, Faryab, Ghazni, Ghor, Helmand, Herat, Jowzjan, Kabul, Kandahar, Kapisa, Khost, Kunar, Kunduz, Laghman, Logar, Nangarhar, Nimroz, Nuristan, Paktika, Paktiya, Panjshir, Parwan, Samangan, Sar-e Pul, Takhar, Uruzgan, Wardak, Zabul

Independence:
> 19 August 1919 (from UK control over Afghan foreign affairs)

National holiday:
> Independence Day, 19 August (1919)

Constitution:
>sixth constitution drafted 14 December 2003 - 4 January 2004; signed 16 January 2004; ratified 26 January 2004

Legal system:
>mixed legal system of civil, customary, and Islamic law

International law organization participation:
>has not submitted an ICJ jurisdiction declaration; accepts ICCt jurisdiction

Suffrage:
>18 years of age; universal

Executive branch:
>chief of state: President of the Islamic Republic of Afghanistan Hamid KARZAI (since 7 December 2004); First Vice President Mohammad FAHIM Khan (since 19 November 2009); Second Vice President Abdul Karim KHALILI (since 7 December 2004); note - the president is both the chief of state and head of government
>
>head of government: President of the Islamic Republic of Afghanistan Hamid KARZAI (since 7 December 2004); First Vice President Mohammad FAHIM Khan (since 19 November 2009); Second Vice President Abdul Karim KHALILI (since 7 December 2004)
>
>cabinet: 25 ministers; note - ministers are appointed by the president and approved by the National Assembly
>
>elections: the president and two vice presidents elected by direct vote for a five-year term (eligible for a second term); if no

candidate receives 50% or more of the vote in the first round of voting, the two candidates with the most votes will participate in a second round; election last held on 20 August 2009 (next to be held on 5 April 2014)

election results: Hamid KARZAI reelected president; percent of vote (first round) - Hamid KARZAI 49.67%, Abdullah ABDULLAH 30.59%, Ramazan BASHARDOST 10.46%, Ashraf GHANI 2.94%; other 6.34%; note - ABDULLAH conceded the election to KARZAI following the first round vote

Legislative branch:

the bicameral National Assembly consists of the Meshrano Jirga or House of Elders (102 seats, two-thirds of members elected from provincial councils for 4-year terms, and one-third nominated by the president for 5-year terms) and the Wolesi Jirga or House of People (no more than 250 seats; members directly elected for five-year terms)

note: on rare occasions the government may convene a Loya Jirga (Grand Council) on issues of independence, national sovereignty, and territorial integrity; it can amend the provisions of the constitution and prosecute the president; it is made up of members of the National Assembly and chairpersons of the provincial and district councils

elections: last held on 18 September 2010 (next election expected in 2015)

election results: results by party - NA; note - ethnicity is the main factor influencing political alliances; composition of Loya Jirga seats by ethnic groups - Pashtun 96, Hazara 61, Tajik 53, Uzbek 15, Aimak 8, Arab 8, Turkmen 3, Nuristani 2, Baloch 1, Pahhai 1, Turkic 1; women hold 69 seats

Judicial branch:
highest courts: Supreme Court or Stera Mahkama; consists of 9 judges

judge selection & term of office: justices appointed by the president with the endorsement of the Wolesi Jirga; justices serve non-renewable 10-year terms

subordinate courts: Cassation and sharia

Political parties and leaders:
note - the Ministry of Justice licensed 84 political parties as of December 2012

Political pressure groups and leaders:
other: religious groups; tribal leaders; ethnically based groups; Taliban

International organization participation:
ADB, CICA, CP, ECO, EITI (candidate country), FAO, G-77, IAEA, IBRD, ICAO, ICC (NGOs), ICRM, IDA, IDB, IFAD, IFC, IFRCS, ILO, IMF, Interpol, IOC, IOM, IPU, ISO (correspondent), ITSO, ITU, MIGA, NAM, OIC, OPCW, OSCE (partner), SAARC, SACEP, SCO (observer), UN, UNCTAD, UNESCO, UNIDO, UNWTO, UPU, WCO, WFTU (NGOs), WHO, WIPO, WMO, WTO

Diplomatic representation in the US:
chief of mission: Ambassador Eklil Ahmad HAKIMI

chancery: 2341 Wyoming Avenue NW, Washington, DC 20008

telephone: [1] (202) 483-6410

FAX: [1] (202) 483-6488

consulate(s) general: Los Angeles, New York

Diplomatic representation from the US:

chief of mission: Ambassador James B. CUNNINGHAM

embassy: The Great Masood Road, Kabul

mailing address: U.S. Embassy Kabul, APO, AE 09806

telephone: [93] 0700 108 001

FAX: [93] 0700 108 564

Key Leaders:

Pres.	Hamid KARZAI
First Vice Pres.	Mohammad FAHIM Khan
Second Vice Pres.	Abdul Karim KHALILI
Min. of Agriculture, Irrigation, & Livestock	Mohammad Asif RAHIMI
Min. of Border & Tribal Affairs	
Min. of Commerce & Industry	Anwar Ul-Haq AHADY
Min. of Communications	Amirzai SANGIN
Min. of Counternarcotics	ZARAR Ahmad Moqbel Osmani
Min. of Defense	BISMULLAH Muhammadi Khan

Min. of Economy	Abdul Hadi ARGHANDIWAL
Min. of Education	Faruq WARDAK
Min. of Energy & Water	Ismail KHAN
Min. of Finance	Omar ZAKHILWAL
Min. of Foreign Affairs	Zalmay RASSOUL, *Dr.*
Min. of Hajj & Islamic Affairs	Mohammad Yusuf NIAZI
Min. of Health	Suraya DALIL, *Dr.*
Min. of Higher Education	Obaidullah OBAID
Min. of Information & Culture	Sayed Makhdum RAHIN
Min. of Interior	Ghulam Mujtaba PATANG, *Lt. Gen.*
Min. of Justice	Habibullah GHALEB
Min. of Martyred, Disabled, Labor, & Social Affairs	Amena AFZALI
Min. of Mines	Wahidullah SHAHRANI
Min. of Public Works	Najibullah AAZHANG
Min. of Refugees & Repatriation	Jamahir ANWARI
Min. of Rural Rehabilitation &	Wais BARMACK

Development	
Min. of Transportation	Daoud Ali NAJAFI, *Dr.*
Min. of Urban Development	Hassan ABDULHAI
Min. of Women's Affairs	Hasan Bano GHAZANFAR
National Security Adviser	Rangin Dadfar SPANTA
Dir. Gen., National Directorate of Security	Asadullah KHALID
Governor, Da Afghanistan Bank	Noorullah DELAWARI
Ambassador to the US	Eklil Ahmad HAKIMI
Permanent Representative to the UN, New York	Zahir TANIN

Flag description:

three equal vertical bands of black (hoist side), red, and green, with the national emblem in white centered on the red band and slightly overlapping the other two bands; the center of the emblem features a mosque with pulpit and flags on either side, below the mosque are numerals for the solar year 1298 (1919 in the Gregorian calendar, the year of Afghan independence from the UK); this central image is circled by a border consisting of sheaves of wheat on the left and right, in the upper-center is an Arabic inscription of the Shahada (Muslim creed) below which are rays of the rising sun over the Takbir (Arabic expression meaning "God is great"), and at bottom center is a scroll bearing the name Afghanistan; black signifies the past, red is for the blood shed for independence, and green can represent either hope for the future, agricultural prosperity, or Islam

note: Afghanistan had more changes to its national flag in the 20th century than any other country; the colors black, red, and green appeared on most of them

National symbol(s):

lion

National anthem:

name: "Milli Surood" (National Anthem)

lyrics/music: Abdul Bari JAHANI/Babrak WASA

note: adopted 2006; the 2004 constitution of the post-Taliban government mandated that a new national anthem should be written containing the phrase "Allahu Akbar" (God is Great) and mentioning the names of Afghanistan's ethnic groups

Chapter 5: Economy

Economy - overview:

Afghanistan's economy is recovering from decades of conflict. The economy has improved significantly since the fall of the Taliban regime in 2001 largely because of the infusion of international assistance, the recovery of the agricultural sector, and service sector growth. Despite the progress of the past few years, Afghanistan is extremely poor, landlocked, and highly dependent on foreign aid. Much of the population continues to suffer from shortages of housing, clean water, electricity, medical care, and jobs. Criminality, insecurity, weak governance, lack of infrastructure, and the Afghan Government's difficulty in extending rule of law to all parts of the country pose challenges to future economic growth. Afghanistan's living standards are among the lowest in the world. The international community remains committed to Afghanistan's development, pledging over $67 billion at nine donors' conferences between 2003-10. In July 2012, the donors at the Tokyo conference pledged an additional $16 billion in civilian aid through 2016. Despite this help, the Government of Afghanistan will need to overcome a number of challenges, including low revenue collection, anemic job creation, high levels of corruption, weak government capacity, and poor public infrastructure.

GDP (purchasing power parity):

$33.55 billion (2012 est.)

country comparison to the world: 109

$30.22 billion (2011 est.)

$28.57 billion (2010 est.)

note: data are in 2012 US dollars

GDP (official exchange rate):

$19.85 billion (2012 est.)

GDP - real growth rate:

11% (2012 est.)

country comparison to the world: 6

5.8% (2011 est.)

8.4% (2010 est.)

GDP - per capita (PPP):

$1,000 (2012 est.)

country comparison to the world: 218

$1,000 (2011 est.)

$900 (2010 est.)

note: data are in 2012 US dollars

GDP - composition by sector:

agriculture: 20%

industry: 25.6%

services: 54.4%

note: data exclude opium production (2011 est.)

Labor force:

15 million (2004 est.)

country comparison to the world: 40

Labor force - by occupation:

agriculture: 78.6%

industry: 5.7%

services: 15.7% (FY08/09 est.)

Unemployment rate:

35% (2008 est.)

country comparison to the world: 182

40% (2005 est.)

Population below poverty line:

36% (FY08/09)

Household income or consumption by percentage share:

lowest 10%: 3.8%

highest 10%: 24% (2008)

Budget:

revenues: $2.243 billion

expenditures: $3.963 billion

note: Afghanistan received $15.7 billion in 2010/2011 (2012 est.)

Taxes and other revenues:

11.3% of GDP (2012 est.)

country comparison to the world: 205

Budget surplus (+) or deficit (-):

-8.7% of GDP (2011 est.)

country comparison to the world: 197

Inflation rate (consumer prices):

13.8% (2011 est.)

country comparison to the world: 210

0.9% (2010 est.)

Commercial bank prime lending rate:
>15.03% (31 December 2011 est.)
>country comparison to the world: 37
>15.69% (31 December 2010 est.)

Stock of narrow money:
>$5.928 billion (31 December 2011 est.)
>country comparison to the world: 93
>$5.307 billion (31 December 2010 est.)

Stock of broad money:
>$6.351 billion (31 December 2011 est.)
>country comparison to the world: 120
>$5.671 billion (31 December 2010 est.)

Stock of domestic credit:
>$363.6 million (31 December 2008 est.)
>country comparison to the world: 178
>$20.06 million (31 December 2007 est.)

Agriculture - products:
>opium, wheat, fruits, nuts; wool, mutton, sheepskins, lambskins

Industries:
>small-scale production of bricks, textiles, soap, furniture, shoes, fertilizer, apparel, food-products, non-alcoholic beverages, mineral water, cement; handwoven carpets; natural gas, coal, copper

Industrial production growth rate:
>NA%

Current account balance:
>-$743.9 million (2011 est.)

country comparison to the world: 106
-$736 million (2010 est.)

Exports:
$376 million (2012 est.)
country comparison to the world: 177
$388 million (2011 est.)
note: not including illicit exports or reexports

Exports - commodities:
opium, fruits and nuts, handwoven carpets, wool, cotton, hides and pelts, precious and semi-precious gems

Exports - partners:
Pakistan 48%, India 19%, Russia 9%, Iran 5% (FY11/12 est.)

Imports:
$6.39 billion (2012 est.)
country comparison to the world: 116
$5.154 billion (2011 est.)

Imports - commodities:
machinery and other capital goods, food, textiles, petroleum products

Imports - partners:
Pakistan 13.7%, Russia 12.6%, Uzbekistan 11.5%, Iran 9.1% (FY11/12 est.)

Reserves of foreign exchange and gold:
$5.268 billion (31 December 2011 est.)
country comparison to the world: 89
$4.174 billion (2010 est.)

Debt - external:

$1.28 billion (FY10/11)

country comparison to the world: 147

$2.7 billion (FY08/09)

Exchange rates:

afghanis (AFA) per US dollar -

51 (2012 est.)

46.75 (2011 est.)

46.45 (2010)

Fiscal year:

21 December - 20 December

Chapter 6: Energy

Electricity - production:
> 913.1 million kWh (2009 est.)
> country comparison to the world: 150

Electricity - consumption:
> 2.226 billion kWh (2009 est.)
> country comparison to the world: 137

Electricity - exports:
> 0 kWh (2010 est.)
> country comparison to the world: 155

Electricity - imports:
> 1.377 billion kWh (2009 est.)
> country comparison to the world: 54

Electricity - installed generating capacity:
> 489,100 kW (2009 est.)
> country comparison to the world: 137

Electricity - from fossil fuels:
> 23.5% of total installed capacity (2009 est.)
> country comparison to the world: 186

Electricity - from nuclear fuels:
> 0% of total installed capacity (2009 est.)
> country comparison to the world: 36

Electricity - from hydroelectric plants:
> 76.5% of total installed capacity (2009 est.)
> country comparison to the world: 18

Electricity - from other renewable sources:
> 0% of total installed capacity (2009 est.)
> country comparison to the world: 100

Crude oil - production:
> 1,950 bbl/day (2012 est.)
> country comparison to the world: 92

Crude oil - exports:
> 0 bbl/day (2009 est.)
> country comparison to the world: 73

Crude oil - imports:
> 0 bbl/day (2009 est.)
> country comparison to the world: 149

Crude oil - proved reserves:
> 87 million bbl (1 January 2012 est.)
> country comparison to the world: 75

Refined petroleum products - production:
> 0 bbl/day (2008 est.)
> country comparison to the world: 119

Refined petroleum products - consumption:
> 4,229 bbl/day (2011 est.)
> country comparison to the world: 176

Refined petroleum products - exports:
> 0 bbl/day (2008 est.)
> country comparison to the world: 148

Refined petroleum products - imports:
> 5,193 bbl/day (2008 est.)

country comparison to the world: 154

Natural gas - production:

30 million cu m (2010 est.)

country comparison to the world: 86

Natural gas - consumption:

30 million cu m (2010 est.)

country comparison to the world: 111

Natural gas - exports:

0 cu m (2010 est.)

country comparison to the world: 150

Natural gas - imports:

0 cu m (2010 est.)

country comparison to the world: 150

Natural gas - proved reserves:

49.55 billion cu m (1 January 2012 est.)

country comparison to the world: 67

Carbon dioxide emissions from consumption of energy:

790,200 Mt (2010 est.)

country comparison to the world: 173

Chapter 7: Communications

Telephones - main lines in use:

13,500 (2011)

country comparison to the world: 199

Telephones - mobile cellular:

17.558 million (2011)

country comparison to the world: 50

Telephone system:

general assessment: limited fixed-line telephone service; an increasing number of Afghans utilize mobile-cellular phone networks

domestic: aided by the presence of multiple providers, mobile-cellular telephone service continues to improve rapidly; the Afghan Ministry of Communications and Information claims that more than 90 percent of the population live in areas with access to mobile-cellular services

international: country code - 93; multiple VSAT's provide international and domestic voice and data connectivity (2012)

Broadcast media:

state-owned broadcaster, Radio Television Afghanistan (RTA), operates a series of radio and television stations in Kabul and the provinces; an estimated 150 private radio stations, 50 TV stations, and about a dozen international broadcasters are available (2007)

Internet country code:

.af

Internet hosts:
>223 (2012)
>
>country comparison to the world: 200

Internet users:
>1 million (2009)
>
>country comparison to the world: 101

Communications - note:
>Internet access is growing through Internet cafes as well as public "telekiosks" in Kabul (2005)

Chapter 8: Transportation

Airports:
    52 (2012)
    country comparison to the world: 91

Airports - with paved runways:
    total: 23
    over 3,047 m: 4
    2,438 to 3,047 m: 4
    1,524 to 2,437 m: 10
    914 to 1,523 m: 2
    under 914 m: 3 (2012)

Airports - with unpaved runways:
    total: 29
    2,438 to 3,047 m: 5
    1,524 to 2,437 m: 12
    914 to 1,523 m: 6
    under 914 m: 6 (2012)

Heliports:
    10 (2012)

Pipelines:
    gas 466 km (2010)

Roadways:
    total: 42,150 km
    country comparison to the world: 85
    paved: 12,350 km

<u>unpaved</u>: 29,800 km (2006)

Waterways:

1,200 km; (chiefly Amu Darya, which handles vessels up to 500 DWT) (2011)

<u>country comparison to the world</u>: 60

Ports and terminals:

Kheyrabad, Shir Khan

Chapter 9: Military

Military branches:
>Afghan Armed Forces: Afghan National Army (ANA, includes Afghan Air Force (AAF)) (2011)

Military service age and obligation:
>22 years of age; inductees are contracted into service for a 4-year term (2005)

Manpower available for military service:
>males age 16-49: 7,056,339
>females age 16-49: 6,653,419 (2010 est.)

Manpower fit for military service:
>males age 16-49: 4,050,222
>females age 16-49: 3,797,087 (2010 est.)

Manpower reaching militarily significant age annually:
>male: 392,116
>female: 370,295 (2010 est.)

Military expenditures:
>1.9% of GDP (2009)
>country comparison to the world: 75

Chapter 10: Transnational Issues

Disputes - international:

Afghan, Coalition, and Pakistan military meet periodically to clarify the alignment of the boundary on the ground and on maps; Afghan and Iranian commissioners have discussed boundary monument densification and resurvey; Iran protests Afghanistan's restricting flow of dammed Helmand River tributaries during drought; Pakistan has sent troops across and built fences along some remote tribal areas of its treaty-defined Durand Line border with Afghanistan which serve as bases for foreign terrorists and other illegal activities; Russia remains concerned about the smuggling of poppy derivatives from Afghanistan through Central Asian countries

Refugees and internally displaced persons:

refugees (country of origin): 2,972 (Pakistan) (2011)

IDPs: 481,877 (mostly Pashtuns and Kuchis displaced in the south and west due to drought and instability) (2012)

Illicit drugs:

world's largest producer of opium; while poppy cultivation was relatively stable at 119,000 hectares in 2010, a poppy blight affecting the high cultivation areas in 2010 reduced potential opium production to 3,200 metric tons, down over 40 percent from 2009; the Taliban and other antigovernment groups participate in and profit from the opiate trade, which is a key source of revenue for the Taliban inside Afghanistan; widespread corruption and instability impede counterdrug efforts; most of the heroin consumed in Europe and Eurasia is derived from Afghan opium; vulnerable to drug money laundering through informal financial networks; regional source of hashish (2008)

Map of Afghanistan

Other Key Facts™ Titles

Key Facts on Syria

Key Facts on China

Key Facts on Qatar

Key Facts on India

Key Facts on Germany

Key Facts on Argentina

Key Facts on Russia

Key Facts on North Korea

Key Facts on Brazil

Key Facts on Italy

Key Facts on the United Arab Emirates

Key Facts on the European Union

Key Facts on Pakistan

Key Facts on Saudi Arabia

Key Facts on Cyprus

Key Facts on Iran

Key Facts on Afghanistan

[Key Facts on Iraq](#)

[Key Facts on Indonesia](#)

[Key Facts on South Korea](#)

All Key Facts™ Titles are Available at www.Amazon.com

THE INTERNATIONALIST®

2013

www.internationalist.com

www.ingramcontent.com/pod-product-compliance
Lightning Source LLC
Chambersburg PA
CBHW071549170526
45166CB00004B/1598